the anxious hippie HANDBOOK

a fun roadmap to finding
the peace, love, & blessings
in anxiety

LUCIE DICKENSON

inspired
girl
BOOKS

The Anxious Hippie Handbook by Lucie Dickenson
Published by Inspired Girl Books
821 Belmar Plaza, Unit 5 Belmar, NJ 07719
www.inspiredgirlbooks.com

Inspired Girl Books is honored to bring forth books with heart and stories that matter. We are proud to offer this book to our readers; the story, the experiences, and the words are the author's alone.

This book is written as a source of information only. The information contained in this book should by no means be considered a substitute for the advice of a qualified medical professional, who should always be consulted before beginning any new diet, exercise, or other health program and before taking any dietary supplements or other medications.

The author and publisher do not assume and hereby disclaim any liability in connection with the use of the information contained in this book.

Products, pictures, trademarks, and trademark names are used throughout this book to describe and inform the reader about various proprietary products that are owned by third parties. No endorsement of the information contained in this book is given by the owners of such products and trademarks, and no endorsement is implied by the inclusion of products, pictures, or trademarks in this book.

ISBN: 978-1-7350944-2-7
Cover design and typesetting by Roseanna White Designs
Cover illustration by Shutterstock
Author photograph by Gorden Dickenson

Library of Congress Control Number:
2020910599

WELCOME

Welcome to your own personal roadmap out of anxiety!

Are you dealing with cray-cray thoughts?

Or paralyzed with fear?

Or maybe you are someone who puts on a good front, so you channel Foxy Cleopatra on the outside, but inside you are scared shitless???

I get it. I was where you were once. Panic attacks were a daily occurrence for me. Weird thoughts seemed to control my mind. I was even carried out of work on a stretcher resulting in a nervous breakdown. My life was out of control. I once shut down a department store because I freaked when I couldn't find my family. No joke. Armed guards and all. So how did I go from wild woman shutting shit down; to peace, love, and can you please pass the cake Lucie?

The lessons are all from my book The Anxious Hippie. These are the exact steps I took to rid myself from years of crippling anxiety. And these lessons I used are all in your Hippie Handbook.

Enjoy the activities, writing prompts and ideas that will get you pumped about learning how to let go of symptoms. But even bigger than getting rid of symptoms (I know zero symptoms seems freaking amazing) is that you will learn how to pull back on the lens of fear and see anxiety in a new light. And once you see it through the lens of peace, love and blessings, there will be no going back!

Remember, you get to choose the narrative for which you see life. ✌️ ♡ ☮

Contents

Lesson 1: Take A Detour 9

Lesson 2: Crowd Out 17

Lesson 3: Fear or Love 24

Lesson 4: Good Morning 32

Lesson 5: I am me 41

Lesson 6: Say hello to my little friend 48

Lesson 7: There is enough 54

Lesson 8: Secrets make you sick 63

Lesson 9: New energy 71

Lesson 10: The Happy Train 79

Lesson 11: Take Out the Garbage 87

Lesson 12: Law of Thirds 95

Lesson 13: Going Fishing? 102

Lesson 14: Acceptance 108

Lesson 15: God Has Got This 116

Lesson 16: These Thoughts 122

Lesson 17: It's in the Genes 129

Lesson 18: Groundhog Day 136

Lesson 19: There's a Party in my Tummy 143

Lesson 20: Get Outside and Go 150

Lesson 21: Setbacks 156

Lesson 22: Imperfect 162

Lesson 23: Sharing Your Smile 168

"Write it down on real paper
with a real pencil.
And watch shit get real"
-Erykah Bodoula

"I am trying to get what
is in my anxious brain down on paper.
The anxiety is the shit.
The real me is under that.
I can't wait to find me again."
-Anxious Response

✌ Hippie Handbook Lesson 1:

Take A Detour

"The shortest distance between two points is a straight line.

If the two points are life and death,

why the heck would I want to go in a straight line?"

We all have an idea on how our life should go. We are told to have goals and dreams. YES!!!! And we can manifest the shit out of those goals and dreams. YES!!!

Most times though there are detours on your journey. These detours are your lessons. It is what is needed to get to the next point. Unfortunately, lessons do not come in rainbow and unicorn packages … in fact mostly they come in the form of symptoms that are trying to get your attention.

My life did not go as I thought it would. There were so many detours I began to think I belonged in the potholes. If I had to draw my journey thus far it would look something like this:

my journey so far....

Now draw your journey. Crayons, pencils. Whatever way you need to express what it has been like for you so far- detours an all... how would that look for you?

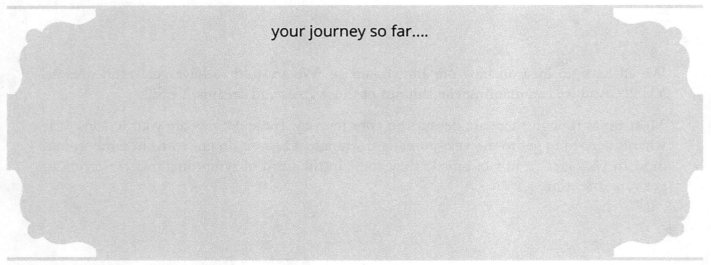

your journey so far....

There are many ways to view these detours on your journey.

You can get upset about them.

Or you can put on a helmet and brace yourself for the ride of your life. It is all about how you choose to see it that creates the experience.

Your life journey is not linear & neither is healing. It is up to you how to experience this ride.

What are your dreams? Your goals? Write about that here

_____
_____
_____
_____
_____
_____

What is the plan that you have for your goals and dreams?

_____
_____
_____
_____
_____

What are the detours you have hit along the way to your goals and dreams?

_____
_____
_____
_____
_____
_____

How do you feel about those detours?

_____
_____
_____
_____
_____

Are feelings the truth? Or are they feelings about how you choose to see something? Can you choose to see the detours in a different light? Is that possible? Maybe? Could there be anything good that came from the detours?

_____

_____

_____

_____

_____

_____

What can you do the next time you hit a roadblock or a detour in your life's plan?

_____

_____

_____

_____

_____

_____

Where is the humor in the detours? How can you see this from the lens of laughter? I chose to see the humor in the ridiculousness of the detours themselves. Every time I found myself in a "ditch" so to speak, I would giggle knowing I was getting ready to level up with some amazing lessons and healing! Where can you see the humor in the detours in your life plan?

_____

_____

_____

_____

_____

Let's freaking wrap this lesson up!

Create up to three hashtags that sum up lesson 1 for you.
For example, in my book, the hashtags I created for this chapter are
#risingup #growth
What are yours??

\# _____

\# _____

\# _____

How are you feeling after that lesson?
Circle what you are feeling right now.
And it can be more than one!
Feelings are just that *feelings*
and they come and go.
Be honest with how you feel and allow yourself
to feel exactly where you are right now...

Feelin'   Feelin'   Feelin'   Feelin'   Feelin'   Feelin'   Feelin'
love   happy   groovy   okay   so sad   down   shit scared

"Everything you've ever wanted is on the other side of fear."

- George Addiar

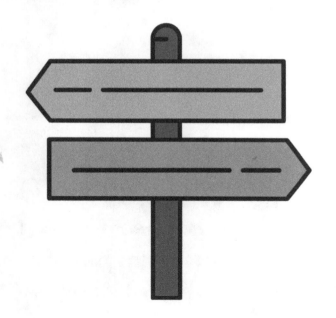

"Can I have directions please?"

-Anxious Response

draw. color. curse.
create. erase.
this is my space to
reflect on this lesson.

take some extra notes...

✌Hippie Handbook Lesson 2:

Crowd Out

"You have more power in the present moment
than any other time in your life. It's your move."

You cannot ever go back and change what happened in the past. It is done.

You cannot be certain of your future… and this can be so very hard for a person dealing with anxiety, because control is the word of the week. Of the year. Of everything. Anxious peeps want control and there is no way to control what already happened or what is going to happen next year. However, there is control – it is found in your own perspective and intention. I know, it sounds so fucking Zen-like, but stick with this….

Make no room in the present moment for anxiety. How? By crowding it out.

When you crowd out anxiety from your life with other thoughts, activities and habits there is no room for the anxiety to hang around.

Anxious thoughts are full of WHAT IF words:

What if I fail the test?

What if my kids don't get home safe?

What if I go crazy?

What if they don't like me?

Here is the secret on how you can crowd out these intrusive, anxious thoughts: by not trying to remove them! Instead fill your mind with what you do want!!! As you change your focus to what you want, instead of what you fear, anxiety quiets down.

Want to try this?

Write in this cloud every shitty thought you have swirling around in your head that makes you feel anxious and/or fearful....

here are my shitty, anxious thoughts.

How does it make you feel when you see this written down?

_____
_____
_____
_____
_____
_____

What do you think the purpose of these thoughts are? Are they helpful to your future and what you want in your life?

_____
_____
_____
_____
_____

Can you be okay with having these anxious thoughts? Can they take a backseat to the thoughts you do want in your life? Write about that.

_____

_____

_____

_____

_____

_____

What are some of the perky things you are thinking of right now? Behind those anxious thoughts? Write out the thoughts that you are loving right now.

here are my thoughts
that I love.

How do these perky joyful thoughts you have written in your pink bubble make you feel? Write about that.

_____

_____

_____

_____

_____

Here is the fun part; write everything from your shitty and perky bubbles below. See how the joyful thoughts can crowd out over the anxious ones? This is how you literally can crowd out anxiety. Oh yes you can!

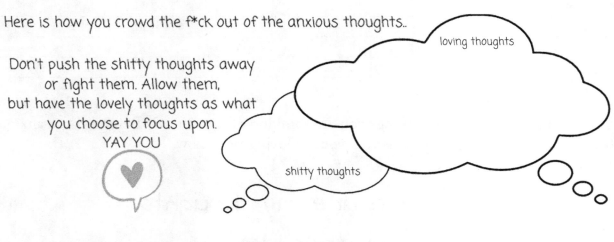

Here is how you crowd the f*ck out of the anxious thoughts..

Don't push the shitty thoughts away or fight them. Allow them, but have the lovely thoughts as what you choose to focus upon. YAY YOU

loving thoughts

shitty thoughts

What can you do the next time your thought bubble is full of anxious thoughts?

_____
_____
_____
_____
_____
_____

Where is the humor in crowding out? How can you see this from the lens of laughter? I was able to see humor in a song. You know that Rush song: "If you choose not to decide, you still have made a choice?" lyric. I learned to laugh; because I knew if I was not choosing the good thoughts, I was still making a choice to let the bad in- and this song would play in my head. Immediately I would giggle and crowd out with good thoughts. Where can you see the humor?

_____
_____
_____
_____
_____
_____

Let's freaking wrap this lesson up!

Create up to three hashtags that sum up lesson 2 for you.
For example, in my book, the hashtags I created for this chapter are
#powerful #letgo
What are yours?

 _____

\# _____

\# _____

How are you feeling after that lesson?
Circle what you are feeling right now.
And it can be more than one!
Feelings are just that *feelings*
and they come and go.
Be honest with how you feel and allow yourself
to feel exactly where you are right now...

Feelin'   Feelin'   Feelin'   Feelin'   Feelin'   Feelin'   Feelin'
love   happy   groovy   okay   so sad   down   shit scared

"If you have good thoughts they will shine out of your face like sunbeams and you will look lovely"
–Ronald Dahl

"If you have scary thoughts, they can freak you out and make you look cray-cray.
Stick with the good thoughts, you will look much better"
– Anxious Response

draw. color. curse.
create. erase.
this is my space to
reflect on this lesson.

✌Hippie Handbook Lesson 3:

Fear or Love

Every cell is listening. What do you want them to hear?

When you hold the vibration of love, your cells are open and receptive to nourishment and health. However, if you hold yourself in the vibration of fear, your cells recoil and close. Every cell in your body responds to your thoughts and your beliefs about the world. Honestly, it sounds a little out there, but you literally are your own doctor. You have the power of how your body will respond and react. Literally.

Is that too much power? Are you ready to take hold of that and fly?? Yes? No? Maybe?

Look at this chart below and maybe it can help you see this even more clearly.

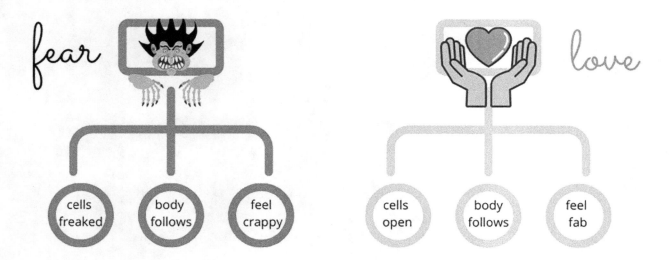

But you might say "I can't control my thoughts! I have scary thoughts!"

We all have scary thoughts, all the time.

It is what you choose to do with the scary thoughts....

Do you get scared of them? Or do you accept them as thoughts and just feel love no matter what?

Okay, shit is going to get real right now.

Write about one of your most anxious thoughts? No need to write anything more.

Just what is that thought?

_____

_____

And how do you feel when you think that thought? Be honest.

_____

_____

_____

_____

_____

_____

Now think about that thought again, but instead can you accept that thought as just a thought and nothing more? Can you just let it go? Write about that and maybe how there is resistance to letting it go?

_____
_____
_____
_____
_____

This can be one of the most difficult hurdles in overcoming anxiety, to see a thought as just a thought. That is why there will be many exercises throughout this journal on this very subject.

BUT let's dive right in. Below is a way to train your brain to see the good and to let go of the shitty thoughts that bring so much unwanted fear into your life.

Below are a couple of word banks. The first is the fear bank. The second is the love bank. Take a look at these words and see how you feel reading each one. Your own personal perspective of every one of these words is creating a chemical reaction in your body by just reading them!

fear word bank

terrified	anxious	alone
threat	alarm	dread
danger	small	risky

love word bank

accepting	calm	connected
safe	joy	beauty
secure	belief	faith

26

How did it feel to read the fearful words? Write about that.

_____

_____

_____

_____

_____

How about those love words? Write about how you feel when you read them?

_____

_____

_____

_____

_____

Now try to search in this word find for ONLY the love words. You may see some of the fear words in this puzzle, they are there on purpose. Don't fucking circle the fear words. Please.

Just notice they are there and move on to find the love words.

```
M V D Z I U A R W G G I A L J T Z G
U D V U O S E I E W B K Z U X H A P
L H R N J F C L U J T R U Z O R W G
C X O E A S E C U R E H G L I E P H
F R P S A C C E P T I N G X S A A A
F T Y C V D X T E H Y X Z T U T D N
Y A V K X E M R C P S B K L Z W S X
W T I C A A R D E T C E N N O C V I
Y R U Z Z I B D T C M J K L G K W O
V R I A F Y E R J S A E E L I O E U
H Q H I E M L I O M H N L I U M M S
E O E K D B I S Y A U O D G L R U U
H D I X N N E K K L Y L V A A N G I
D T X C Y Q F Y M L S A C L L C K D
D X I O V K I G X Y E T A K R C H L
F H K A D A N G E R X X R N D H R K
Z S I Z F K P H V W P X M C G W E M
M X G T X W F O F S O B Z Y X C S V
```

Did you find all the love words? So sorry if you didn't because there is not a key! 😊

Anyway, the love words are the things you focused on finding, even though the fear words are there. You did not focus on them. You can do the same with anxiety. Focus on what makes you feel love and pay no mind to the anxious fearful thoughts. Write about this exercise.

_____

_____

_____

_____

_____

Do you think you can try now to do that in your own mind? To ignore the fearful anxious thoughts that are whirling around in your brain and latch onto the beautiful words that make your heart sing? Write about that.

_____

_____

_____

_____

_____

Where is the humor in the fear or love for your cells? How can you see this from the lens of laughter? Can you see that there is humor in there somewhere? I imagined my cells talking to me like the little Whos on the wish flower from Horton Hears a Who. Remember, they were yelling "We are here! We are here! We are here!" Your cells are yelling at you the same way about your thoughts. It always makes me laugh a little to think of it this way. What makes you find humor in this one?

_____

_____

_____

_____

_____

Let's freaking wrap this lesson up!

Create up to three hashtags that sum up lesson 3 for you.
For example, in my book, the hashtags I created for this chapter are
#feedyourcells #therightfood
What are yours?

\# _____

\# _____

\# _____

How are you feeling after that lesson?
Circle what you are feeling right now.
And it can be more than one!
Feelings are just that *feelings*
and they come and go.
Be honest with how you feel and allow yourself
to feel exactly where you are right now...

Feelin' Feelin' Feelin' Feelin' Feelin' Feelin' Feelin'
love   happy   groovy   okay   so sad   down   shit scared

"WHAT YOU FEED YOUR MIND DETERMINES YOUR APPETITE."
-TOM ZIGLAR

"FEED MYSELF GOOD THOUGHTS AND IGNORE THE FEARFUL ONES. GOT IT. MY APPETITE LIKES CHOCOLATE CAKE THOUGH. CAN I FEED MY MIND SOME CAKE?"

draw. color. curse.
create. erase.
this is my space to
reflect on this lesson.

✌Hippie Handbook Lesson 4:

Good Morning

"Every morning is a new start.
Heck, every second is a new start."

Every morning holds infinite possibilities. A sunrise is a reminder for you that you can leave the past where it belongs and to begin every day in the energy of newness. Please hold the knowledge that you are not stuck. Ever. You have the power to change at every single moment. You hold that much power!

So today is a great day to manifest the shit out of what you want!!

It is also a good day to let go of what you don't want …

You have only so much time on this earth…and it is important to remember that.

Why the heck would I put this in a handbook about anxiety???

Wouldn't this just freak someone with fear the fuck out? Probably not.

Because people who deal with anxiety are some of the most intelligent people in the world and it is insulting to tip-toe around the obvious. If you do nothing to change your ways about anxiety, time still marches on and hours turn into days that turn into years.

Stick with this.

You got this.

Allow yourself to get over anxiety once and for all so you can spend all your minutes doing what you want to do instead of having freaking panic attacks!

how many mornings do you want to continue waking up anxious?

Today is the day you created yesterday, right???

So, what you do today will create your tomorrow. Make sense?

What do you want tomorrow to look like? And I don't mean tomorrow in the sense "your life and all its tomorrows", I actually mean what do you want tomorrow to look like? Like the day after today? Write about that:

What I want tomorrow to look like:

_____

_____

_____

_____

_____

_____

And while we are talking about it, what don't you want to bring into your tomorrow?

_____

_____

_____

_____

_____

_____

_____

Okay it is nice to write down what you want it to look like, but that is just a dream right now.

It is time for action. What can you do to make the list above come true? Here is a plan of action sheet for you to fill out every day to make it all happen

Make sure you fill it out every morning and night, and really try hard not to miss a day!

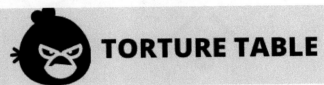

TORTURE TABLE

What I want	Ideas on how to get there	Signs of progress

WTF???

I know the LAST thing you want to do is keep a fucking record of your progress.

LOL!! Of course, this is not an exercise. Remember? I had anxiety at one time too and I know the LAST thing I wanted to do was to fill out anything long term. I was looking for quick tips and something to stop the freaking symptoms. I understand that filling out a table would seem like running a marathon right now. Cross out that table and write whatever you want all over it.

You don't need no stinkin' table!

Instead place your focus, every night before you go to sleep and every morning when you wake up, upon what you want. And then go out and do those things; and bring the fear with you. Literally bring it along with you and invite it to go with you wherever you go. As you do that fear loses its edge, because you are in control instead of fear controlling you. Kinda cool, huh?

Write about how you think this can be helpful to healing from anxiety

_____

_____

_____

_____

_____

While we are at it, how about you draw a picture of your fear? What would it look like?

Is it just a blob of color? A monster type thing? Or is it something entirely different? Did you ever see Monsters Inc, the Disney movie? Remember Boo's drawing of Randall? Does it look something like that? Draw what you think your fear looks like here in this circle:

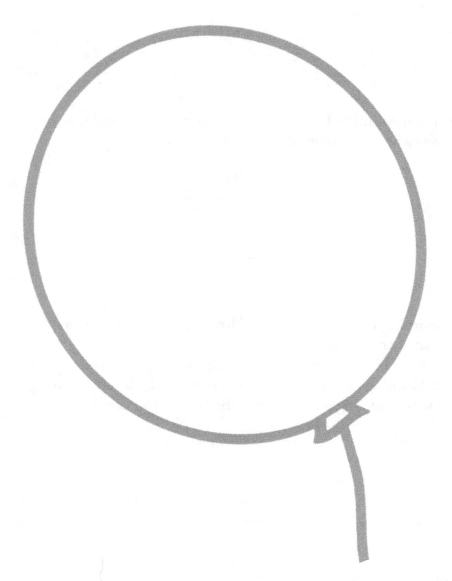

Now that you see it; know you can just take that along with you wherever you go. Imagine your fear in this circle with a string, like a balloon, and it is light and weightless. You may have it with you, but it is not of you. It is outside of you in this balloon and it is not weighing you down at all. And it does not have control of you. In fact, if you want; you can let go of the balloon and let it float away....

Write about what your fear looks like and how the imagery of placing your fear in a balloon feels like. Do you think it is helpful for you? Write about that here:

_____

_____

_____

_____

_____

_____

Have you missed out on anything in your life because you have been too scared? Can you flip the script and instead go everywhere you want and bring fear with you?

_____

_____

_____

_____

_____

_____

Where is the humor in every morning being a new start? How can you see this from the lens of laughter? Can you see that there is humor in there somewhere? The way I saw the humor was every morning in my head I heard Gene Kelly and Debbie Reynolds from Singing In The Rain singing "Good Morning" It was so silly and cheesy and I loved replaying this every morning … it would make me giggle… Where is the humor you can find?

_____

_____

_____

_____

_____

Let's freaking wrap this lesson up!

Create up to three hashtags that sum up lesson 4 for you.
For example, in my book, the hashtag I created for this chapter is
#lettinggo
What are yours?

\# _____

\# _____

\# _____

How are you feeling after that lesson?
Circle what you are feeling right now.
And it can be more than one!
Feelings are just that *feelings*
and they come and go.
Be honest with how you feel and allow yourself
to feel exactly where you are right now...

Feelin' love	Feelin' happy	Feelin' groovy	Feelin' okay	Feelin' so sad	Feelin' down	Feelin' shit scared

"EVERY TIME YOU ARE TEMPTED TO REACT IN THE SAME OLD WAY, ASK IF YOU WANT TO BE A PRISONER OF THE PAST OR A PIONEER OF THE FUTURE."
-DEEPAK CHOPRA

"i JUST WANT TO FEEL NORMAL RIGHT NOW AND NOT HAVE SWEAT STREAMING DOWN MY BOOBS.
-ANXIOUS RESPONSE

draw. color. curse.
create. erase.
this is my space to
reflect on this lesson.

take some extra notes...

✌Hippie Handbook Lesson 5:

I am me

"You are not your diagnosis.

The diagnosis is not you.

Believe. Rinse. Repeat."

When you get a diagnosis such as anxiety; sometimes you might forget it is just a label.

Anxiety is not who you are. If you identify yourself as your diagnosis, how can you ever let go of it??? Your current health is not who you are; it is just a benchmark for where change may be needed. How cool is it that your body alerts you to such important needs???

Can we just rip this name tag off please and instead let's listen to a little Eminem and hear his music? You know the one:

Hi my name is (what)

My name is (who)

Who are you??? Well the deep Zen answer is something along the lines of you are simply love. And I believe that, I really do. (most days, sometimes I forget) But the question is, do you believe that? If not, or if you are not sure, there is definitely more crud to wash off to uncover the true you.

Think of the words you may use to describe yourself. What are the words that you are using?

Most of the time these descriptive words begin with the phrase "I Am"

So, go ahead begin

I AM_____. You fill in the blank.

Write all the words you want in this cloud. Try to use positive words like I am love. I am connected. I am joyful. Whatever it is put it in this pretty, fluffy cloud.

How do those words you just wrote make you feel? Write about that here

_____
_____
_____
_____
_____

These positive statements are wonderful because the energy of the words "I AM" creates reinforcement and ownership. It is super powerful. However, the issues arise when we use "I AM" for negative self-talk or stress talk. Without realizing it every day we say I am _____. And fill that blank with something negative. How about I am anxious? Or I am sick? Or I am weak? Or I am angry.

Fill in I Am _____ in the cloud below with all the negative things you may unknowingly be assigning ownership to.

These are words we don't want to take on personally as identity, as they are not the truth of who you are, but instead they are descriptive words of how you are feeling. Of course, it is okay to feel sick, but you don't want to be sickness. Your subconscious mind listens, and will adjust accordingly to the words you feed it.

How do those negative words you just wrote make you feel? Write about that here

_____
_____
_____
_____
_____

So, going forward be aware of I AM statements and instead use I FEEL statements. This simple change takes away ownership and replaces it with a fleeting feeling.

Words are so powerful. Use them to create goodness, kindness and love. Always when you are talking about yourself, because you are the biggest advocate for you. And remember, you are not your diagnosis!

Take a moment and see how you feel today. Write about that now using the start I FEEL...

_____

_____

_____

_____

_____

Do you see that those feelings are not you, but literally just a feeling?

Okay, we are going deep here... knowing what you now know- who are you?

_____

_____

_____

_____

_____

_____

Write about how this exercise may have made you think about your words? What might you change going forward?

_____

_____

_____

_____

_____

_____

Where is the humor in your identity? How can you see this from the lens of laughter? Can you see that there is humor in there somewhere? The way I saw the humor in it was to absolutely laugh at what words I could completely and lovingly assign to myself that make me giggle like I am supercalifragilisticexpialidocious or I am a freaking fashion icon diva .... Where is the humor you can find?

_____

_____

_____

_____

Let's freaking wrap this lesson up!

Create up to three hashtags that sum up lesson 5 for you.
For example, in my book, the hashtag I created for this chapter is
#perfectlyimperfect
What are yours?

 _____

\# _____

\# _____

How are you feeling after that lesson?
Circle what you are feeling right now.
And it can be more than one!
Feelings are just that *feelings*
and they come and go.
Be honest with how you feel and allow yourself
to feel exactly where you are right now...

Feelin'   Feelin'   Feelin'   Feelin'   Feelin'   Feelin'   Feelin'
love   happy   groovy   okay   so sad   down   shit scared

"The question isn't who is going to let me; it is who is going to stop me."
-Ayn Rand

"It was me. I get it. I was being a pain in the ass to myself. I AM healing now."
-Anxious Response

draw. color. curse.
create. erase.
this is my space to
reflect on this lesson.

Hippie Handbook Lesson 6:

Say hello to my little friend

"Healing is an inside job.

No one is coming to save you.

But you my friend, you can help save yourself."

It is 100% your job to get yourself better.

Not your spouse, family, doctor, energy healer therapist, friend… whoever… not their job.

It is yours. Of course, you may need help, we all do. We are not meant to be on our journey alone, but it is ultimately you that needs to do the work.

No more pity parties. I mean how does that help your anxiety? It just keeps you stuck in it.

No more blame. Again, not trying to be a dick but honestly placing blame ultimately means you believe that someone has power over you. Think about it, if you are blaming them for not healing you, you must think they have power over you and that, my friend, takes your power away.

Stop that stinking thinking! You absolutely have the power inside of you right now to get well.

be the star in your life movie, not anxiety

Take your power back and be the active main character in your life and healing.

How? Here are a few examples:

- Every day tell yourself 10 freaking awesome things that you love about yourself.
- Get up, get dressed and get out.
- Crowd out your negative thoughts with what you do want
- Take anxiety with you. You are in control, not anxiety

Try to find 5 more ways you can be the active main character in your healing.

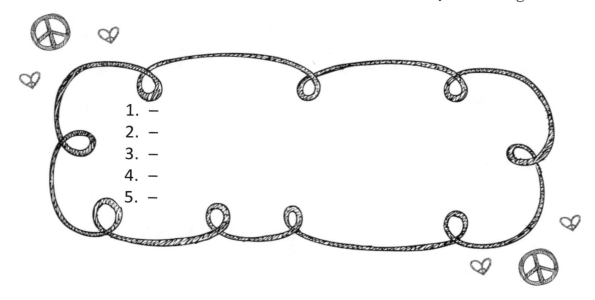

1. —
2. —
3. —
4. —
5. —

Here is the tagline from my business: Anxiety can be your greatest blessing.

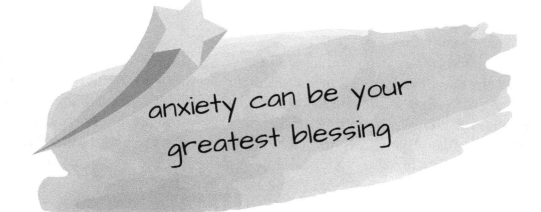

anxiety can be your greatest blessing

I have this tagline because I truly believe these words. There is nothing within you that needs fixing, because you are not broken. It is a remembering of who you are and what you are made of that is the big lesson here.

Can you create a tagline for your anxiety healing? Something that will get you motivated to kick ass and move forward? Write it in here....

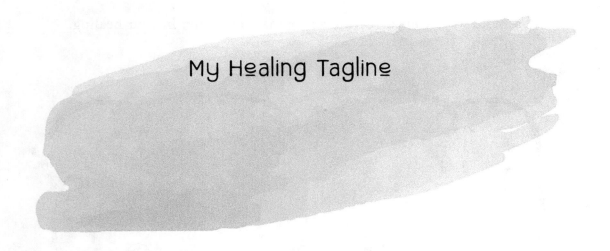

My Healing Tagline

How does this tagline make you feel? Does it empower you? Write about that.

_____
_____
_____
_____
_____
_____

Where is the humor in knowing you have all the power to heal within you? How can you see this from the lens of laughter? Can you see that there is humor in there somewhere? The way I saw the humor in it was to laugh at the irony that I spent $100, 000 to find an answer to anxiety, when all along it was within me. If I didn't laugh about this, I would be sitting in the middle of my floor crying uncontrollably. And to honest, some of the shit I did during those healing years was freaking hysterical. Like getting stuck to wax in my bathroom and my husband having to come home and de-wax me. (story in my book lol) Where is the humor you can find?

_____
_____
_____
_____
_____
_____

Let's freaking wrap this lesson up!

Create up to three hashtags that sum up lesson 6 for you.
For example, in my book, the hashtags I created for this chapter are
#ikindalikemenow #thepoweriswithin
What are yours?

\# _____

\# _____

\# _____

How are you feeling after that lesson?
Circle what you are feeling right now.
And it can be more than one!
Feelings are just that *feelings*
and they come and go.
Be honest with how you feel and allow yourself
to feel exactly where you are right now...

Feelin'	Feelin'	Feelin'	Feelin'	Feelin'	Feelin'	Feelin'
love	happy	groovy	okay	so sad	down	shit scared

"Woe-is-me is not an attractive narrative"
- Maureen Dowd

"Agreed. My new narrative is to go back to the places that I was scared-and laugh so hard and love so much that fear has no fucking clue what to do."
-Anxious Response

draw. color. curse.
create. erase.
this is my space to
reflect on this lesson.

✌Hippie Handbook Lesson 7:

There is enough

"It is safe to shine."

We all were made to shine.

You are meant to shine brightly, without strings attached or conditions. It is your own beliefs that you hold (many times subconsciously) that can limit you. These limiting beliefs create a ceiling for just how much greatness you can achieve. Let go of what does not serve you and understand that each of you hold the abundance of the world within. When will you accept that greatness???

Sometimes we may begin to shine, but when we see competition around us, we get small again. And then the anxiety starts up. You may believe that there is not enough light for everyone and that you will be squeezed out of your piece of the glory. Bullshit! You are meant to shine right up there with everyone else. Your star is just as bright as the one next to you!!!

it is safe to shine
come out from behind the
clouds

Let me stop here and say the next few journal entries work so much better when you are *completely* honest and choose to be real and get it all out. Not just a little. All of it. Remember no one is viewing this but you. This is your safe space. Get out what is inside, because it is a needed step in getting over anxiety. If you think someone is an asshole; write that. If you think you are being a jealous wanker, write that. Get it out. Honestly it is time to see it all. When you see it, you can heal it! YAYAYAYAYAY!

Write your thoughts about stepping out and shining bright here? Does the idea of shining scare you? Do you get freaked out when someone else is shining? Do you shrink? Write about all of that here.

_____

_____

_____

_____

_____

_____

Look at what you just wrote above. Are there clues to beliefs you may be holding? Write about how you could look at yourself and others shining differently?

_____

_____

_____

_____

_____

_____

OKAY! Now that we got that out, let's dig deep into you....

Shining is your birth right.

As we grow older, we tend to hide parts of ourselves that we believe others may not find acceptable. We shrink. We hide. We change. And in this process, we lose ourselves.

Unfortunately, we do this for so long- we hide those parts- we forget who we really are.

Let's go back to when you were a child and bring out all that you loved and what brought you joy. Bring out that little kid inside that had dreams filled with confidence, silliness and laughter. It is time to stop taking it all so seriously. Be who you are. As you begin to once again allow all those true colors to shine, anxiety takes a hike.

CAN YOU REMEMBER?

Close your eyes. Go back and remember what those things were that you always wanted to do. Or possibly you are doing those things right now, but you are hiding from the light. See yourself shining brightly in your mind's eye. Stay there for a few minutes and notice how you feel. When you are done take a deep breath and write down exactly what you saw and how you wish to shine in life. Remembering you!

Remembering Me

- _____
- _____
- _____
- _____

- _____
- _____
- _____
- _____

Sometimes anxiety likes to take hold right now, because it knows that you are understanding this process and moving away from anxiety and into self-love! Please don't give in!!! And if you do, no worries, because you know how to get back to center now right? Crowding out, eyes on your goal, ignoring anxious thoughts, standing in your light…. Right? Stay with me ….

If you are thinking about how fabulous you are (and you are!!!) doubt can creep in now and you may think this is all just pretend. That this happy shit may work while writing in the journal, but in the "real world" you are not that fabulous and possibly see yourself as a fraud! That everyone else has their life together while you are just scrambling to stay sane! Here is a little secret. No one in this world has all their shit together. You are amazing and no one can deliver your gifts and your message the way that you can. That is why there is no need to be intimidated by anyone. Ever. There is always enough room in this world for you and your message. You are uniquely you and that message from you is needed.

Please fill in the blank to add words to your self-love word bank! No need to write in a straight line. Write all over inside and outside the box!

I am so freaking fabulous!
Here are a few words about me
and why I am meant to shine!

Can you see just how needed you are to shine bright in this world? Your very talents are not only beautiful, but gifts from God to give to the world. Write about how that makes you feel?

_____

_____

_____

_____

_____

How does this lesson resonate with you? What did you learn about yourself? Write about that here.

_____

_____

_____

_____

_____

Where is the humor in knowing you are a shining star? How can you see this from the lens of laughter? Can you see that there is humor in there somewhere? The way I saw humor in this lesson was to imagine myself little again and have a day where I did everything my "little girl" wanted to. I would jump in puddles and sing in the rain at the top of my lungs. Sometimes with my kids, sometimes alone! It was a remembering of what made me smile and the way I could shine. And do you know on those days my anxiety level was incredibly low??!! Where is the humor you can find in this lesson?

_____

_____

_____

_____

_____

Let's freaking wrap this lesson up!

Create up to three hashtags that sum up lesson 7 for you.
For example, in my book, the hashtag I created for this chapter is
#shinebrightlikeadiamond
What are yours?

\# _____

\# _____

\# _____

How are you feeling after that lesson?
Circle what you are feeling right now.
And it can be more than one!
Feelings are just that *feelings*
and they come and go.
Be honest with how you feel and allow yourself
to feel exactly where you are right now...

Feelin' love	Feelin' happy	Feelin' groovy	Feelin' okay	Feelin' so sad	Feelin' down	Feelin' shit scared

59

"A jewel is just a rock put under enormous heat and pressure. Extraordinary things are always hiding in places people never think to look."
- Jodi Picoult

"Look in my head. With all the anxiety pressure, there should be a fuck-load of diamonds in there. Just kidding! I am an diamond in the rough ready to shine!"
- Anxious Response.

draw. color. curse.
create. erase.
this is my space to
reflect on this lesson.

take some extra notes...

✌Hippie Handbook Lesson 8:

Secrets make you sick.

"Throw it up, get it out.
It may be gross, but just think-
that was inside of you."

We all have something in our past that we have hidden. Could be a trauma. A secret. Or even a burden that is not even yours, but you are holding it for any number of reasons. Whatever it is… it is not your job to carry it. Even beliefs that you have created in your subconscious mind need to be purged if they are limiting and outdated.

By keeping all of that low energy stuff inside, you are hurting you. And the longer it stays inside of you, the more anxiety you may experience. Anxiety is challenging you, like a bully. And just like a bully it does not think that you will stand up to it. Anxiety expects you to recoil, suffer with symptoms and keep all the secrets inside. But remember, that is not who you are- you are a shining amazing person and you have held this crap long enough! Stand up to the bully aka anxiety and show it you are no longer taking its shit. Or holding shit. Or hiding shit.

If you feel like this is a good space for you now to get it out- write below all the things you wish to purge. Old beliefs. Old secrets. Pent up emotions. Go ahead and let it fly .

Purge it all in the space under GET OUT on the next page. LOL.

GET OUT

How do you feel about what you wrote above? Write about that here

_____
_____
_____
_____
_____
_____

What can your next step be to help you make sure you got it all out? What does that look like to you? Is it therapy? Coaching? Energy Healing? More journaling? Prayer? Write about that here

_____
_____
_____
_____
_____
_____

In case you have more to say, by all means go for it!

On the next page there is more space for you to get it out!

GET OUT

How did this lesson help you see how anxiety can be nudging you to help yourself? Can you see that at all?

_____
_____
_____
_____
_____
_____

Remember you are made of love and light. There is nothing needed to hold inside any longer. You are here for this amazing ride we call life; experience it in health, exactly as God intended. Let go!

You were never meant to be a container full of shit.

You are a vessel of love & kindness. Keep yourself clean inside and out.

I am worthy of a healthy body & mind

Do you feel worthy of health? Of letting go of anxiety completely? What would that feel like to you? Who would you be without anxiety? Talk about that here.

_____
_____
_____
_____
_____

Where is the humor about secrets making you sick? How can you see this from the lens of laughter? Can you see that there is humor in there somewhere? I literally got stuff out when I went for high colonics and hummed a tune with my hubby when it was over... "Mr. Clean. Mr. Clean" We literally roared laughing. Healing can be funny! How can you see humor in this????

_____
_____
_____
_____
_____

Let's freaking wrap this lesson up!

Create up to three hashtags that sum up lesson 8 for you.
For example, in my book, the hashtags I created for this chapter are #nooneisperfect #weareallalittledirty
What are yours?

_____

_____

_____

How are you feeling after that lesson?
Circle what you are feeling right now.
And it can be more than one!
Feelings are just that *feelings*
and they come and go.
Be honest with how you feel and allow yourself
to feel exactly where you are right now...

Feelin' love   Feelin' happy   Feelin' groovy   Feelin' okay   Feelin' so sad   Feelin' down   Feelin' shit scared

"What lies behind you and what lies in front of you pales in comparison to what lies within you."
- Ralph Waldo Emerson

"What the heck is within me?
I want to get that shit out.
And then get to know and trust the me that has been underneath it all."
-Anxious Response

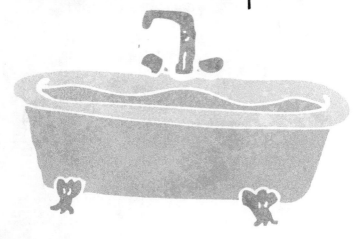

draw. color. curse.
create. erase.
this is my space to
reflect on this lesson.

take some extra notes...

✌Hippie Handbook Lesson 9:

New energy

"No one told me growth included outgrowth."

To get well from anxiety, it is imperative to look at the person who is perpetuating it. I didn't say caused it. No one knowingly causes anxiety for themselves. What I am saying is the person that keeps the anxiety fire alive day after day, is you.

When you see yourself as you are; mistakes, miracles and messy movement forward you become honest with all the ways you have been holding yourself back. Maybe you thought it was safer to stay where you are than to venture into the unknown? Or maybe you feel that you deserve to be where you are, all mixed up in anxiety? Or even you just don't know where to start to find your way out? There could be a number of reasons for why you stay in the constant loop of anxiety, but whatever the reason, now is the time to see things a little more clearly. To remove the fog and see the truth in front of you. You are now learning how to remove the clouds so you can clearly see YOU!

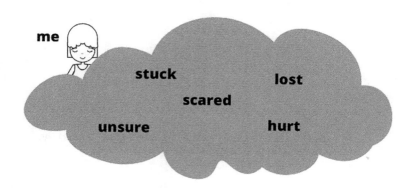

How does it feel knowing that there may be something you are holding onto that may be keeping you stuck? Write about that.

_____

_____

_____

_____

_____

When you start to let go of the darkness and step into the light; your entire energy will shift. You become a vibrational match for the light you are now sending out. Fortunately, that means new exciting healing ventures, new people and new habits ahead. However, it can also mean the ending to things which no longer serve you, like relationships that have run their course.

God, the Universe, Love; whatever name you give to your foundation of goodness in this world (and beyond) has such a bigger plan for you. Allow the changes to happen. It is healthy to move forward. And it beautiful to be thankful for what was, and knowing full well it may be time to let that go.

Take some time for this lesson's exercise. You may have to come back to it again and again. Write from your heart and what it truly wants. This may be ridiculously emotional- that is good! Emotions are fabulous. Allow them. Feel them. Continue writing. This is a beautiful undoing and becoming process…. Anxiety is going to shit right about now… because you are not allowing anxiety to have your focus… your focus is now on you!!!!!

what am I looking forward to entering my life…..

what am i holding onto that maybe could go……

After you have filled in the above, about what you wish to leave your life and what you are looking forward to entering your life, write about what you see written and how you feel about that.

_____

_____

_____

_____

_____

This energy shift is necessary to move forward and letting go of things that have held you back is hard. But remember, you cannot catch the blessings today if your hands are full of yesterday's weight. Okay?

At this point, are you feeling like anxiety is a little more removed from your focus? Or ramping up harder? Write about that here.

_____

_____

_____

_____

_____

Where is the humor about moving forward and letting go and outgrowth? How can you see this from the lens of laughter? Can you see that there is humor in there somewhere? My humor was in literally laughing out loud every time I had the courage to let go of something in my life and seeing how freaking quickly a blessing would pop up. Like literally just fucking pop up. The Universe was waiting for me to get my shit straight!!! How can you see humor in this????

_____

_____

_____

_____

_____

_____

Let's freaking wrap this lesson up!

Create up to three hashtags that sum up lesson 9 for you.
For example, in my book, the hashtags I created for this chapter are
#growingup #growingout #growingin
What are yours?

\# _____

\# _____

\# _____

How are you feeling after that lesson?
Circle what you are feeling right now.
And it can be more than one!
Feelings are just that *feelings*
and they come and go.
Be honest with how you feel and allow yourself
to feel exactly where you are right now...

Feelin' love	Feelin' happy	Feelin' groovy	Feelin' okay	Feelin' so sad	Feelin' down	Feelin' shit scared

"You can never cross the ocean until you have courage to lose sight of the shore."
-Anonymous

"Baby steps, dude. Let me try crossing the street without a panic attack first. But I will get there."
-Anxious Response

draw. color. curse.
create. erase.
this is my space to
reflect on this lesson.

take some extra notes...

✌Hippie Handbook Lesson 10:

The Happy Train

"To be happy all the time
Would be so exhausting, right?"

When you are dealing with anxiety well-meaning people say some really silly shit. Right up there at the top of shit peeps may say to you is "Just be happy."

WTF? Okay. Thanks. I didn't think of that. I will get right on it. LOL

Of course, they are trying to help. And you know if you could just "be happy" you would, but it is not possible to be happy all the time. And not just for a person dealing with an anxiety condition. No one is happy all the time. But in our happy obsessed world we hear messages like:

If you get in shape, you will be happy.

If you eat chocolate you will be happy (I believe this one 😂)

If you have many friends you will be happier

If you do what you love, you will be really happy.

Write about some ways you were told if you did _____ then you will be happy. And does that spark anxiety in any way?

_____

_____

_____

_____

_____

_____

Happy is not a constant state. And striving for that sets us up to feel awful because we can't reach this Utopian state of bliss at all times. Write about how you feel when you or someone else tells you to "just be happy" or to "just feel calm."

_____

_____

_____

_____

_____

We have a range of emotions. And each emotion can be accepted and honored.

Happy is one. Scared is another. Both are okay. Try not to judge one over the other.

Of course, we want more happy, just like more cowbell.

Of course we want more happy, just like we want more cowbell

But if you have fear and are not happy in the present moment, allow it to hang out for as long as it wants. Because it is fleeting and will leave in time to be replaced by other emotions. Pay it no mind, but don't fight it and begrudge it because it is not happiness.

How does allowing fear to stay and inviting it in feel for you? Is that scary? Write about that.

_____

_____

_____

_____

_____

When happiness does come greet it with open arms and allow it to stay and pay mind to it. Feed it your attention. Write about how you can keep positive emotions with you for longer periods of time.

_____

_____

_____

_____

_____

_____

Get that cowbell out because this lesson is all about music....

If you're happy and you know it,
clap your hands!
If you're happy and you know it,
clap your hands!
If you're happy and you know it,
and you really want to **grow** it;
If you're happy and you know it,
clap your hands.!

Then try it to "stomp your feet."
And "nod your head."
You can even shout "Hooray!"
and if you're really up for it,
you can do all of them.

When you are happy try this, you know this song from childhood. Sing it at the top of your lungs!!!

But again, happy isn't every moment and you can't just count the minutes between happy time, you need to live in those minutes no matter how you feel! And that will create happiness....

This may seem hokey, but it works! When you stand up to anxiety in a way that is not a fight, you calm the alarm bells in your head. I know you want to run or fight, because every instinct is telling you to fight. But how has that been working for ya? Try something different. Dancing and singing in the face of fear is a different way to approach anxiety... see what happens when you do....

If you're scared and you know it,
laugh out loud!
If you're scared and you know it,
laugh out loud!
If you're scared and you know it,
and you really want to **expose** it;
If you're scared and you know it,
laugh out loud!

Then try it to "shake your butt."
And "wave your hands."
You can even shout "My way!"
and if you're really up for it,
you can shout and laugh until fear is gone.

Did you try this? Write about how what happened. If you did not try this, why? Is it too easy? Sometimes the silly, easy ways are the secret passages to healing....

_____

_____

_____

_____

_____

Where is the humor about the happy train? How can you see this from the lens of laughter? Can you see that there is humor in there somewhere? I learned to laugh like a hyena at anxiety when it came on. It was amazing how quickly the shift from anxious to calm did happen. How can you see humor in this????

_____

_____

_____

_____

_____

Let's freaking wrap this lesson up!

Create up to three hashtags that sum up lesson 10 for you.
For example, in my book, the hashtags I created for this chapter are
#itsokay #tbh #iammostlyhappy
What are yours?

\# _____

\# _____

\# _____

How are you feeling after that lesson?
Circle what you are feeling right now.
And it can be more than one!
Feelings are just that *feelings*
and they come and go.
Be honest with how you feel and allow yourself
to feel exactly where you are right now...

Feelin' love	Feelin' happy	Feelin' groovy	Feelin' okay	Feelin' so sad	Feelin' down	Feelin' shit scared

Be happy. Not because everything is good, but because you can see the good side of everything.
-Anonymous

Yep.
Seeing the humor and the blessing in anxiety;
and that creates happiness.
-Anxious Response

draw. color. curse.
create. erase.
this is my space to
reflect on this lesson.

take some extra notes...

Hippie Handbook Lesson 11:

Take Out the Garbage

"Allowing in the negative pollutes the soul."

Negativity is everywhere. So is positivity. We tend to attract like energy, right? Like attracts like.

If you are scared and surround yourself with negative things, that fear is being sent out into the world in an energetic form to everyone and everyplace you go. And even more fascinating, is that same fearful energy you put out into the world comes back to you again and again. Because the Universe gives you exactly what you ask for. And by taking in negative and focusing on negative- that is your signal to the Universe of what you want. So, the Universe gives you more of that. Kinda cool, right???? Take a look at the picture below. On the left side is what it can be like when you immerse yourself in the negative. It is like you shouting from a megaphone.

Not the beacon you want to be sending right? On the flip side if you are a floating Zen master your energy send out will look something like the right side of this picture. A calm lotus flower pulsing love though the world. And that love-fest will come back to you ten-fold!

Most of us are somewhere in-between the two, vacillating back and forth, trying to figure it all out.

Where do you think you fall in between the two different messages? Are you more someone who lives in fear and live in that all day? Or do you thank everything that comes your way? Talk about that here.

_____

_____

_____

_____

_____

_____

How can we get more like Zen Lotus person and away from Foghorn Fear person?

The first step is to take note of what you are letting into your life.

It is so very easy to fall into the trap of negativity. It is everywhere from the moment you wake up to the moment you shut your eyes. And even when you try to sleep, your daily events replay in your head. Take note for your own health where you want to set boundaries.

Here are some examples of what we all can be letting in every day:

Negative news. Negative gossip. Negative time wasters (technology). Negative food.

Now that you have ideas on what you may be letting in every day that is negative, fill that in here:

where are you letting
in the pollution?

1.

2.

3.

Take a look at what you wrote in the pollution cauldron. Do you see some places in your life where you could set a boundary to not let so much negative in? Write about that here.

_____
_____
_____
_____
_____

Next, take note of the positive that you let in every day

where are you letting
in the positive?

1.

2.

3.

How can you let more of those things in every day? Write about that here.

_____
_____
_____
_____
_____
_____

A great way to begin letting the light into your life is to begin a gratitude list. You literally can change the direction of your life with this beautiful list because once again you are training your brain to focus upon your blessings. When you focus on what you are grateful for, there is space from the fight and/or flight surging through your system, and your nerves have an opportunity to calm down.

Start a gratitude list now! List ten things you are grateful for and this list need not be anything earth shattering. This is not a competition; it is a realization. There are so many things to be grateful for!!

Things I Am Grateful For

1. _____
2. _____
3. _____
4. _____
5. _____
6. _____
7. _____
8. _____
9. _____
10. _____

As you continue to complete a gratitude journal, you again crowd out anxiety and you are moving more towards Zen Lotus person … woo-hoo!!! You are freaking awesome!

Where is the humor in "taking out the garbage"? Or not letting in the poison? How can you see this from the lens of laughter? Can you see that there is humor in there somewhere? I had a blast with this one because I did not watch the news for years and if I went to turn on the television, I only watched funny shows and movies. Okay maybe I watched the Notebook a dozen times, with my husband next to me. And I may or may not have cried every time. But we giggled together after every cry, because he said I had Notebook amnesia and forgot every time how emotional I got. Anyway, much better than news on a loop! How can you see humor in this????

_____
_____
_____
_____
_____

Let's freaking wrap this lesson up!

Create up to three hashtags that sum up lesson 11 for you.
For example, in my book, the hashtags I created for this chapter are
#positive #or #polution
What are yours?

\# _____

\# _____

\# _____

How are you feeling after that lesson?
Circle what you are feeling right now.
And it can be more than one!
Feelings are just that *feelings*
and they come and go.
Be honest with how you feel and allow yourself
to feel exactly where you are right now...

| Feelin' love | Feelin' happy | Feelin' groovy | Feelin' okay | Feelin' so sad | Feelin' down | Feelin' shit scared |

"You can't litter negativity everywhere and then wonder why you've got a trashy life."
-Anonymous

"Cleaning up my mess. Learning to make my true home sparkle."
– Anxious Response

draw. color. curse.
create. erase.
this is my space to
reflect on this lesson.

take some extra notes...

# Hippie Handbook Lesson 12:

Law of Thirds

"Do they like me? Is not the question.

Do you like you? That is the one to answer."

When dealing with anxiety, many often worry if every person in the world likes them or not.

Dealing with anxiety is tough enough, but to carry the weight of everyone's opinions around is too fucking heavy. Let that shit go. I know. I know. It is easier said than done. It is because so many have been conditioned to base their worth on other people, rather than what is inside

How do you feel when you read this first paragraph? Does this ring true for you? Write about that here.

_____

_____

_____

_____

_____

I was given some epic advice once and I will pass that on to you

"Not everyone is going to like you. Stop wasting your time on those that don't."

This man went on to tell me his unofficial science of the law of thirds.

He said one-third of everyone likes you, one-third of people do not like you and the last third don't even know you or care.

It is not personal. This is not about you. It is about them. Stay out of it 🚭

What other people think about you is none of your business. And if the insecurity of it becoming your business creeps in; remember the law of thirds. It is such a great reminder. God puts exactly who is supposed to be in front of you at exactly the right time. He makes no mistakes. Let that be. Don't worry about the other two thirds. They have their own shit going on. Stay out of it.

Not everyone's journey intersects with your journey. And that is okay. We can all have a different path to walk AND still vibrate love and kindness to all.

The law of thirds. How do you feel about this? What is coming up for you? Write about that.

_____
_____
_____
_____
_____

Do you ever find yourself worrying about what you said to someone and how they are judging that? Or do you worry if someone is gossiping about you? What if you tried not even to think about that? What if it just didn't bother you? Write about that.

_____
_____
_____
_____
_____

Let's get off the topic of everyone else right now and just focus on you. Because it is what you think of you that is important!!! Fill out the list below and please fill out all ten things you love about yourself...

10 THINGS I ♥ about me

1

2

3

4

5

6

7

8

9

10

Look at the list and the beautiful words you wrote about yourself? How do those words make you feel?

_____

_____

_____

_____

_____

Can you see now that it is YOU that needs to feel the love for YOU? When you feel that for yourself other people's opinions won't matter. Write about that.

_____

_____

_____

_____

_____

Where is the humor about the law of thirds? How can you see this from the lens of laughter? Can you see that there is humor in there somewhere? It was very hard for me to find humor in this one for a long time, but as I continued my healing journey I finally got to a point where I would laugh at the truth of the law of thirds. I would energetically send every person, no matter if they liked me or not, a vibe of love. As I did this, I laughed at how small minded I was to believe everyone had to be my friend. It is not about that. It is about love and kindness. How can you see humor in this????

_____

_____

_____

_____

_____

Let's freaking wrap this lesson up!

Create up to three hashtags that sum up lesson 12 for you.
For example, in my book, the hashtags I created for this chapter are
#lawofthirds #itsokay
What are yours?

\# _____

\# _____

\# _____

How are you feeling after that lesson?
Circle what you are feeling right now.
And it can be more than one!
Feelings are just that *feelings*
and they come and go.
Be honest with how you feel and allow yourself
to feel exactly where you are right now...

Feelin'   Feelin'   Feelin'   Feelin'   Feelin'   Feelin'   Feelin'
love   happy   groovy   okay   so sad   down   shit scared

I do not care so much what I am to others as I care what I am to myself."
-Michel de Montaigne

"I see. Like me. Then send that love out."
– Anxious Response

draw. color. curse.
create. erase.
this is my space to
reflect on this lesson.

✌Hippie Handbook Lesson 13:

Going Fishing?

"I used this more than anything else in
helping me overcome anxiety."

A fish is lured in by bait.

You are also lured in- by your anxious thoughts.

When anxiety hooks you; you struggle just like a fish that has been caught.

The trick is not to get hooked. Right?

But how the heck can you stay off the bait that is so freaking tempting to grab???

The trick is to swim around the bait.

Can you understand how you hook your thoughts by giving them attention?

Write about that here.

_____

_____

_____

_____

_____

What thoughts are the ones that hook you the most?

Write them below:

where do you take the bait?

When you see the way anxiety can grab onto you and have you hook onto those specific thoughts you wrote about above, can you see that you are literally hooked on anxiety?

How do you feel when you get hooked? What happens mentally and physically?

Instead of getting hooked onto your anxious thoughts, you now know you can swim around the bait. How? I start you off with a couple ways, can you add more that would work for you?

WAYS TO NOT FREAKING HOOK ON!

1. Literally say to yourself when you feel the thoughts coming "don't take the bait"

2. Allow the thoughts to be there, but begin to do something else

3. Write in this journal

4. _____

5. _____

6. _____

Can you now see that it is you that has the power? You have the choice to take the bait of the anxious thoughts or swim around them. The more you hook on, the more you will struggle with anxiety. Write about what you learned in this chapter.

_____
_____
_____
_____
_____
_____

Where is the humor about not taking the bait? How can you see this from the lens of laughter? Can you see that there is humor in there somewhere? When I would be up in the middle of the night, drenched in sweat from yet another panic attack I would laugh out loud thinking of myself as a trout taking the bait. This gave me the pause I needed to remember not to hook on!

How can you see humor in this????

_____
_____
_____
_____
_____
_____

Let's freaking wrap this lesson up!

Create up to three hashtags that sum up lesson 13 for you.
For example, in my book, the hashtags I created for this chapter are
#swimaroundit #power
What are yours?

\# _____

\# _____

\# _____

How are you feeling after that lesson?
Circle what you are feeling right now.
And it can be more than one!
Feelings are just that *feelings*
and they come and go.
Be honest with how you feel and allow yourself
to feel exactly where you are right now...

Feelin'	Feelin'	Feelin'	Feelin'	Feelin'	Feelin'	Feelin'
love	happy	groovy	okay	so sad	down	shit scared

You don't have to control your thoughts. You just have to stop letting them control you.
-Dan Millman

Okay, I get it. By me giving them attention, they are hooking me. I am going to just keep swimming from now on.
- Anxious Response

draw. color. curse.
create. erase.
this is my space to
reflect on this lesson.

Hippie Handbook Lesson 14:

Acceptance

"The key to healing is acceptance
The lock is you."

THIS IS A BIGGIE!

If you accept it all. Everything. The whole fucking mess.

You have won.

How? Because when you accept everything, you are no longer fighting it.

Acceptance in the present moment is your springboard for change.

How can you change something if you don't admit it is there?

I am not saying to push it down and forget about it. True acceptance is found
in the statement:

I TRULY LOVE MYSELF, WITH OR WITHOUT THIS ANXIETY

Can you see what acceptance is really about? It is not about *wanting* anxiety and the reasons
for it, but instead about accepting that you *may or may not be* anxious and accepting the
reasons anxiety manifested, and loving yourself no matter what.

Can you write about your thoughts about accepting yourself? No matter what?

_____
_____
_____
_____
_____
_____

Now it is your turn. The simple act of putting pen to paper and writing this out is helping your brain change some outdated ideas and habits about self- love.

Write it out however you wish. As long as the meaning is you love yourself no matter what. Try writing it many different ways below...

Read what you wrote. How does that make you feel? Can you see that acceptance is such a big part of surrendering to anxiety, which in turn will make it subside? Write about that

_____
_____
_____
_____
_____

Can you find one of the ways you wrote how to accept yourself and make that your mantra? Or form a mantra from that statement? Write about that mantra? How does it make you feel?

_____
_____
_____
_____
_____

When you accept all the STUFF that may have happened and the baggage that came along with that STUFF that happened, you win. Because it releases YOU!!!

Accept the bag of shit you have been carrying around. It is there anyway! Once you acknowledge it, you are in a place to let it go!

This next exercise is to be done with:

No pencil or crayons. No writing.
Just you and yourself. Opening the door to healing.

Can you take a moment and sit in a quiet space?

Relax your shoulders. Your jaw. Your face. Your arms. Your legs.

And can you give yourself permission to just be fully relaxed?

Close your eyes (after reading this LOL) and when you do close them, begin to take a slow deep breathe in--------and then out. And then please do that again- a slow deep breath in-----and out.

And imagine all the STUFF you have dragged around with you for years in a cute pink duffle bag. (in my meditation it is a pink duffle, whatever you want to be carrying this shit in is fine. I guess 😂)

Can you look at that bag of STUFF and accept it? Right now. Accept the fact that you have been dragging it around and it is with you. I am not saying you have to like it or jump up and down like a maniac that you have it... asking you to just accept it is with you right now. No fighting it. No hating it. Just seeing it for what it is. A bag of shit.

You have a choice right now. Do you want to open the bag of shit and play with it in your meditation and bring it with you into tomorrow????? Or do you want to say goodbye to it? Your choice... (God I hope you are not choosing to play with it- but if so, please make believe wash your hands)

As you say goodbye to it and you release that weight you were carrying around, can you give yourself permission to walk into the next moment without it? Really see yourself without it. Can you allow that? And as you are allowing that can you watch yourself walk away from it? And watch as the bag gets smaller and smaller until you can no longer see it?

Now take a deep breath. And come back to your new moment in time. Weighing a little less.

Welcome!!! You rock!

How did that meditation work for you?

_____

_____

_____

_____

_____

As you accept everything EXACTLY as it is in the moment. You are able to springboard forward into change… WOO HOO!!!!

Where is the humor about acceptance? How can you see this from the lens of laughter? Can you see that there is humor in there somewhere? Of course, my way is the pink shit bag! Makes me laugh every time!! How can you see humor in this????

_____

_____

_____

_____

_____

Let's freaking wrap this lesson up!

Create up to three hashtags that sum up lesson 14 for you.
For example, in my book, the hashtags I created for this chapter are #accepteverything #eventhesymptoms
What are yours?

\# _____

\# _____

\# _____

How are you feeling after that lesson?
Circle what you are feeling right now.
And it can be more than one!
Feelings are just that *feelings*
and they come and go.
Be honest with how you feel and allow yourself
to feel exactly where you are right now...

| Feelin' love | Feelin' happy | Feelin' groovy | Feelin' okay | Feelin' so sad | Feelin' down | Feelin' shit scared |

"Many never realize they always had the key in their pocket, so they die at the locked door, never reaching deep inside to pull it out."
-Anthony Liccione

Not dying. Living..
I opened the door!
-Anxious Response

draw. color. curse.
create. erase.
this is my space to
reflect on this lesson.

✌ Hippie Handbook Lesson 15:

God Has Got This

"Thank you
I couldn't hold it all."

Anxiety is about control. And wanting to control it all, can kinda make you feel

like you are alone. But you are never alone. You are always connected to love.

God -Love- Source-Nature Goddess-The Universe would like nothing better than to help you with anxiety. Holding onto your shit and believing you can control it is an impossible task. Give it to God. It is okay to share your shit with God.

I think He pretty much knows what to do with it -lol.

Trust & Faith.

These two words are why sometimes we hoard our problems and try to control them.

Because maybe we don't have trust or faith in too many things or people?

What comes up for you when the words trust & faith are mentioned? Do you trust and/or have faith in others? In love? Write about that:

_____

_____

_____

_____

_____

_____

Here is the thing. The root of anxiety has so many different reasons. Everyone has their own unique root for why they started feeling anxious; be it trauma, disease, deficiencies, diet, beliefs, fearful thinking, stress, hormones (and so many more). But what if love (God) was actually giving you a gift in healing from anxiety??? Like, really... what if we all had different reasons for anxiety starting, but we all get the same gift in healing...

What if anxiety was actually a gift?
A blessing?

teaching trust & faith? strength & acceptance? self-love and connection?

How does this make you feel when you read anxiety can be a blessing? Mad? Angry? Relief? Disbelief? Happy? Write about that here.

_____

_____

_____

_____

_____

_____

Can you think of any gifts that you may have received BECAUSE of anxiety and your quest to get well? Fill in the box below with those gifts...

What gifts & lessons have you been given BECAUSE of anxiety?

When you read the gifts that you wrote down, how does that now make you feel? About anxiety? About love? About blessings?

_____

_____

_____

_____

Maybe shitty things in our life don't have a good reason for why they happen? Or maybe you believe everything has a reason? Regardless of what you believe as to the WHY you got anxiety, can you see that just maybe, God steps in and turns the crappy stuff in our life into opportunities to see the light within?

When you change your cry from help me to thank you, your whole freaking world changes! Miracles begin to happen in your healing.

What have you learned about yourself? About others? About faith and trust because of anxiety?

Write about that here.

_____

_____

_____

_____

_____

Where is the humor about giving it to God? How can you see this from the lens of laughter? Can you see that there is humor in there somewhere? I laughed every time I thanked God and imagined Him literally in everything. Especially chocolate! How can you see humor in this????

_____

_____

_____

_____

_____

Let's freaking wrap this lesson up!

Create up to three hashtags that sum up lesson 15 for you.
For example, in my book, the hashtags I created for this chapter are
#faith #trust #miracles
What are yours?

_____

_____

_____

How are you feeling after that lesson?
Circle what you are feeling right now.
And it can be more than one!
Feelings are just that *feelings*
and they come and go.
Be honest with how you feel and allow yourself
to feel exactly where you are right now...

| Feelin' love | Feelin' happy | Feelin' groovy | Feelin' okay | Feelin' so sad | Feelin' down | Feelin' shit scared |

"Search for God.
You will find
HIM in everything."
-Julie Jenifer

"Even in anxiety? Really?
Well I guess maybe... because anxiety
kind of forced me look
within and grow.
So yeah, God is in anxiety.
And I ALWAYS knew
He was in chocolate cake! YUM!!"
-Anxious Response

draw. color. curse.
create. erase.
this is my space to
reflect on this lesson.

✌ Hippie Handbook Lesson 16:

These Thoughts

"Just because you have a thought
doesn't mean it is true."

The anxious brain pumps out thoughts. Scary thoughts. Weird thoughts. Terrifying thoughts.

But it is not just anxious peeps that have negative thoughts, everyone does. Every day. People without an anxiety issue can quickly discard negative thoughts and pay them zero attention.

However, when you feel anxious, you tend to examine the thoughts. You try reason with them. You fight them because sometimes they are so disgusting you want to rid yourself of them and get them out of your head. When you do this over and over again, you begin to build a pathway in your brain telling your brain "this thought is dangerous, let's keep an eye on it when it comes again!"

That is how Automatic Negative Thoughts are formed. Automatic Negative Thoughts (ANTS) can be so engrained in the anxious mind that you don't even know they are happening.

ANTS
fuck off

Just like in life when you see one ant, you know there are more... same with **a**utomatic **n**egative **t**houghts! You may not know you have them, but they are the first thoughts that pop up causing a fear & danger response in your thinking.

Can you understand how ANTS happen? Do you notice that in your anxious thinking patterns? Write about that here.

_____
_____
_____
_____
_____
_____

Automatic negative thoughts get people suffering with anxiety really scared, because these thoughts come seemingly out of the blue. This sudden thought popping in your head can really freak you out because you can't understand why you are thinking these cray-cray thoughts. And instead of ignoring them, you fall into the pattern of trying even harder to fight them, which just reinforces the pathway for this to happen again.

Here's the real deal.

The secret weapon. Ignore ANTS.

Just because you have a thought, doesn't make it true.

Let me say that again…

Your anxious thoughts are not a truth!

So, next time you have a thought in your head that is making you hop, skip and jump all over the house and causing wild panic symptoms, remember these ANTS. These little fuckers. They are just a learned response. That's it. Nothing more.

Yes, it is okay to look at them, even say hello to them. You just don't want to fight them.

Invite them in right now and see them for what they are. Just thoughts. Not a truth.

Can you think about the thoughts that create panic for you?? Write about those here.

_____
_____
_____
_____
_____

Is it possible that these thoughts that you wrote about above are just ANTS? Can you write to your ANTS in the box below? What do you want to say to them?

Dear ANTS,

You can reprogram your mind to not have these ANTS! Just remember to not pay these thoughts mind.

Next time you get a thought in your brain that tries to scare you and wants to engage with it, can you remember what you wrote above to your ANTS?

_____
_____
_____
_____
_____

Where is the humor about acceptance? How can you see this from the lens of laughter? Can you see that there is humor in there somewhere? I loved the movie Bug's Life and I saw the ANTS as the BIG mean bugs in the movie and saw me as the little guy that defeated them. I laughed every time I would watch the movie! How can you see humor in this????

_____
_____
_____
_____
_____

Let's freaking wrap this lesson up!

Create up to three hashtags that sum up lesson 16 for you.
For example, in my book, the hashtags I created for this chapter are
#justathought #notatruth
What are yours?

\# _____

\# _____

\# _____

How are you feeling after that lesson?
Circle what you are feeling right now.
And it can be more than one!
Feelings are just that *feelings*
and they come and go.
Be honest with how you feel and allow yourself
to feel exactly where you are right now...

Feelin'   Feelin'   Feelin'   Feelin'   Feelin'   Feelin'   Feelin'
love   happy   groovy   okay   so sad   down   shit scared

"Great minds discuss ideas; average minds discuss events; small minds discuss people."
-Eleanor Roosevelt

And anxious minds discuss everything. Inside their heads. Loudly. Looking forward to kicking out ANTS.
-Anxious Response

draw. color. curse.
create. erase.
this is my space to
reflect on this lesson.

take some extra notes...

✌ Hippie Handbook Lesson 17:

It's in the Genes

*"Breaking the hurts of the past
clear a way for the future."*

Okay. How's it going so far??? Good? Great.

Because we are going to get into some really wild stuff here and just going to blurt it out:

Sometimes your anxiety is not yours.

Well, it's yours, but it didn't begin with you.

WTF?????

You know how you get your eye color and weird pinky toe from your genes???

What do you think about also inheriting some emotional baggage that others in your lineage forgot to let go of???

Generational issues need not be something that keeps getting passed down from generation to generation.

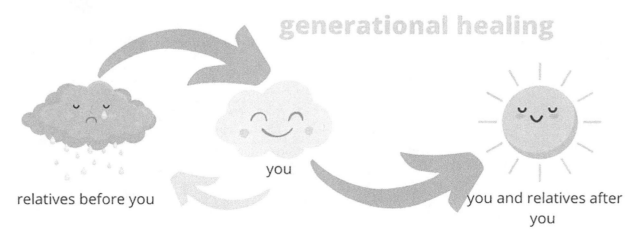

generational healing

relatives before you · you · you and relatives after you

This is a lot to take in. Write about how you are feeling about generational healing so far...

_____

_____

_____

_____

You do not have to be the hero and heal EVERYTHING for everyone in your family. That is not your fucking job! Ever! But you can chip away at these generational issues simultaneously while healing your own anxiety.

When we hold a grudge. When we hold hate. When we hold rage. When we hold blame.

It is us that suffers. And those feelings seep way down inside ourselves and literally change our chemistry. And that chemistry is passed on to the next generation and so on...

What is the secret ingredient to healing these issues?

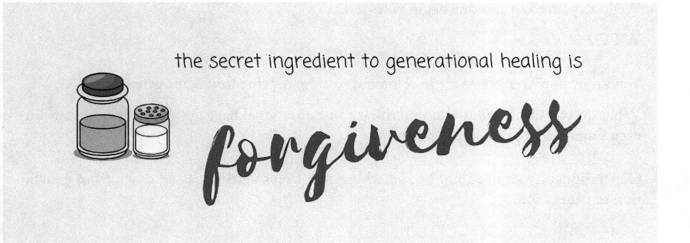

the secret ingredient to generational healing is

forgiveness

Forgiveness is extremely personal, and finding the way that works for you to let go is part of this amazing journey. A few ways that come to mind are energy healing, tapping, prayer, therapy, meditation. Sometimes it is as simple as writing it down and getting it out. I will give you space here to do just that. But how do you forgive for past generations? By putting your intentions on not just you, but on all those that came before you. And when you are forgiving, ask your body to release it all. Everything. All that you are holding. Not just your stuff, but the stuff that generations before have held. If you have the urge to write, do it here in this space. Write whatever comes to your mind, no matter how cray-cray the thoughts are about. When you set your intentions on healing generations, there can be some really wild things that come up. Allow that to come up and get out. As you write here, you may feel a big release…

Forgive

What did you think about this lesson? Do you see how this can help with healing from anxiety? Write about that here.

_____

_____

_____

_____

_____

_____

Where is the humor in forgiveness? How can you see this from the lens of laughter? Can you see that there is humor in there somewhere? I would say Please Excuse My Dear Aunt Sally every time I was healing from one of these generational things. Because I wanted to use what I learned in math somewhere in healing- lol! How can you see humor in this????

_____

_____

_____

_____

_____

_____

Let's freaking wrap this lesson up!

Create up to three hashtags that sum up lesson 17 for you.
For example, in my book, the hashtag I created for this chapter is
#breakinguptheband
What are yours?

_____

_____

_____

How are you feeling after that lesson?
Circle what you are feeling right now.
And it can be more than one!
Feelings are just that *feelings*
and they come and go.
Be honest with how you feel and allow yourself
to feel exactly where you are right now...

| Feelin' love | Feelin' happy | Feelin' groovy | Feelin' okay | Feelin' so sad | Feelin' down | Feelin' shit scared |

Forgiveness is a funny thing. It warms the heart and cools the sting.
-William Arthur Ward

And removes the bees. Figuratively of course. We love bees.
-Anxious Response

draw. color. curse.
create. erase.
this is my space to
reflect on this lesson.

Hippie Handbook Lesson 18:

Groundhog Day

"For circumstances to change,
you have to take action to make a change."

Someone once told me this:

The first time you live through it,
Is on them and/or the problem
Every other time you relive it, it is on you.

Learning you are breathing life into the very thing that hurts you is hard to take.

Sometimes we have to breathe life into it to heal it.

But we definitely do not need to sit in it and live there!

Does this make sense to you? Is there anything that you continuously repeat again and again that you know is not for your highest and best good? Write about that here.

_____

_____

_____

_____

_____

_____

_____

Take back your power! No longer allow anyone or anything that happened to steal your joy.

Ask yourself this: What do you want to breathe life into instead??? Fill that in the bubble below!

What do you want to breathe life into?

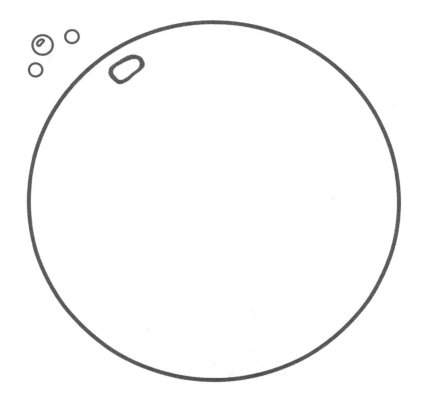

When you see what you DO want to have in your life and what you HAVE been allowing in, can you see how anxiety may have been actually been a blessing, teaching you to focus on what you want in life?

_____

_____

_____

_____

_____

_____

You are so incredibly amazing and have so many gifts to give yourself and this world. Try not to let things go on repeat like Groundhog Day (the movie) because you have so much more to offer this world than staying stuck!!!

Take action to create change! How? Take at least one step every day in the direction of what it is that you do want. Sometimes the most you can do is get out of bed and get dressed. But maybe the next day you start a new hobby, or begin a new class. And you can take fear with you if it wants to come...

what you do want?

1.

2.

3.

4.

Write about ways you can take steps to get to where you do want to go

_____
_____
_____
_____
_____
_____

You got this keep going!!! You are freaking doing this!

Where is the humor in this Groundhog Day lesson? How can you see this from the lens of laughter? Can you see that there is humor in there somewhere? If I found myself doing something that was keeping me stuck in the past, I did my best Bill Murry imitation and said

"In the immortal words of Jean-Paul Sartre: 'Au revoir, gopher!'"

How can you see humor in this????

_____
_____
_____
_____
_____

Let's freaking wrap this lesson up!

Create up to three hashtags that sum up lesson 18 for you.
For example, in my book, the hashtags I created for this chapter are
#healthy #thatwasmygoal
What are yours?

\# _____

\# _____

\# _____

How are you feeling after that lesson?
Circle what you are feeling right now.
And it can be more than one!
Feelings are just that *feelings*
and they come and go.
Be honest with how you feel and allow yourself
to feel exactly where you are right now...

| Feelin' love | Feelin' happy | Feelin' groovy | Feelin' okay | Feelin' so sad | Feelin' down | Feelin' shit scared |

"The past does not equal the future unless you live there."
-Tony Robbins

"Moving out of that place in the past. Getting a new residence."
- Anxious Response

draw. color. curse.
create. erase.
this is my space to
reflect on this lesson.

take some extra notes...

✌Hippie Handbook Lesson 19:

There's a Party in my Tummy

"What you feed yourself is everything.
Thoughts. Food. Faith."

What you eat. What you think. What you believe.

It is all food. Nourishment.

For your body. For your mind. For you soul.

The previous lessons have gone into great detail on how to nourish your mind & soul.

But what about food for the body?

What you eat can probably give you one of the quickest results in getting over anxiety.

It is not to say that eating well will solve everything, because healing from anxiety is about the harmony and peace holistically. But…changing your habits around food definitely can show extremely quick symptom reduction.

It is super simple. Eat nutrient dense whole foods.

Go freaking wild on fruits & veggies

Eat much less of or eliminate entirely processed foods.

Test for food allergies and sensitivities.

Try to let go of sugar and caffeine while healing from anxiety.

You Got This Shit!
(Just don't eat too much of this shit)

How is your diet right now? Does it match up with this picture? Are you eating good, whole food?

Write about your current diet here.

_____

_____

_____

_____

_____

_____

If you are eating sugary treats and a pot of coffee every day, your adrenaline is going to jump into overdrive and give you those classic anxiety symptoms. Your blood sugar will be all over the place. And your sleep may be off because of it. But even beyond sugar and caffeine, everything you eat can impact your brain (and the rest of your body). The gut-brain connection is real and something everyone with anxiety can investigate to see how their diet creates symptoms.

Aside from coffee, sugar and processed food; another thing to look for is what food makes you not feel good or bloats you. Sometimes food can be responsible for brain fog and even the really scary anxiety symptoms like racing thoughts and feeling like you are going to pass out. For me, when I gave up gluten and dairy, it was like a miracle. So many anxiety symptoms went away. For you it may be gluten and dairy too or it may be different foods. That is why you need to investigate this because there is not one answer for everyone.

A food journal for ten days is a perfect snapshot for you to uncover the correlation between diet and anxiety. This is a super quick way to literally see for yourself the result of the food you are nourishing your beautiful body with and how it affects you physically, emotionally and yes even spiritually.

Can you see how food can have a direct impact on you and the result can be anxiety? How does that make you feel? Empowered? Angry? Something else? Write about that here.

_____

_____

_____

_____

_____

_____

Use this food journal as a guideline to see how you can track every day what you eat, your mood that day and any symptoms. Also, you want to track your elimination. That is right, your poop lol!

Because if your poop is not right, it means something is going on in your gut and that can be a clue into symptoms. Use this every day!

Yummy Stuff — My Food Journal

WHAT I ATE	HOW I FELT	SYMPTOMS	BATHROOM	NOTES

Write about what you have noticed between what you eat and anxiety symptoms.

_____

_____

_____

_____

_____

_____

Where is the humor in this nutrition lesson? How can you see this from the lens of laughter? Can you see that there is humor in there somewhere? If you read my book you know that at one point, I could only eat five foods. My gut was a mess. I had to laugh or I would be freaking crying! My humor from this was the name of this lesson "There is a party in my tummy" – and I would sing this song from the show "Yo Gabba Gabba". If you don't know the song or video, it is definitely worth looking up and singing along! How can you see humor in this????

_____

_____

_____

_____

_____

_____

Let's freaking wrap this lesson up!

Create up to three hashtags that sum up lesson 19 for you.
For example, in my book, the hashtag I created for this chapter is
#foodforthought
What are yours?

\# _____

\# _____

\# _____

How are you feeling after that lesson?
Circle what you are feeling right now.
And it can be more than one!
Feelings are just that *feelings*
and they come and go.
Be honest with how you feel and allow yourself
to feel exactly where you are right now...

Feelin'   Feelin'   Feelin'   Feelin'   Feelin'   Feelin'   Feelin'
love   happy   groovy   okay   so sad   down   shit scared

"To keep the body in good health is a duty... otherwise we shall not be able to keep our mind strong and clear."
–Buddha

"Anxiety is teaching me so much about how to be the best me!"
–Anxious Response

draw. color. curse.
create. erase.
this is my space to
reflect on this lesson.

Hippie Handbook Lesson 20:

Get Outside and Go

"Exercise was and still is a lifeline for me."

Exercise is your best friend. Really. It is magic for helping kick anxiety out of your life.

Many times, you are so very tired from all the symptoms, the mental drain and the lack of sleep that the last thing you want to do is go out and exercise, but please make the effort.

Because getting outside into the air (yes outside!) is so healing, grounding and beneficial for your mental and physical health.

What types of exercise are you doing now? Daily? Weekly? Write about that here

_____

_____

_____

_____

_____

There are so many different ways you can begin to exercise! And you can make it more interesting by switching it up every day. Here are just a few examples of ways that you can get your exercise in daily. I am certain you can immediately think of other ways you can get exercise too!

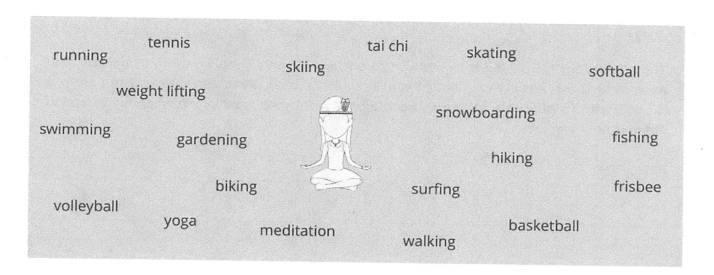

running tennis tai chi skating softball
skiing
weight lifting snowboarding
swimming gardening fishing
hiking
biking surfing frisbee
volleyball
yoga basketball
meditation
walking

If you notice there are many forms of exercise on this list including aerobic, strength, flexibility, balance. When you exercise, feel-good endorphins are released which can take you out of the stress cycle and into the "I feel freaking awesome" cycle.

Also, on this list there are mind-body exercises listed. When you meditate, practice yoga or tai chi (or any other mind-body exercise which can actually be almost anything on this list too!) you are quieting the active anxious brain and instead focusing upon the present moment. Over time you learn to stay more in the "now" and less time in worrying about the future.

How can you incorporate all types of exercise; including mind-body into your daily schedule?

Write about that here.

_____

_____

_____

_____

_____

_____

The exercise for this lesson is to literally go out and exercise!!! So, go do that! Because you want to kick this anxiety crap out of your life and exercise is such an easy way to help you rid yourself of symptoms. When you come back from your exercise, write about what you did and how you feel

_____

_____

_____

_____

_____

_____

Where is the humor in exercising? How can you see this from the lens of laughter? Can you see that there is humor in there somewhere? There were so many times I felt just too tired to do anything, let alone go out an exercise. But I would play the Rocky theme in my head (and sometimes even wear a black knit hat like him) and go out and do it! How can you see humor in this????

_____

_____

_____

_____

_____

_____

Let's freaking wrap this lesson up!

Create up to three hashtags that sum up lesson 20 for you.
For example, in my book, the hashtag I created for this chapter is
#walkandmeditate
What are yours?

_____

_____

_____

How are you feeling after that lesson?
Circle what you are feeling right now.
And it can be more than one!
Feelings are just that *feelings*
and they come and go.
Be honest with how you feel and allow yourself
to feel exactly where you are right now...

Feelin' love   Feelin' happy   Feelin' groovy   Feelin' okay   Feelin' so sad   Feelin' down   Feelin' shit scared

"Good things come to those who sweat."
Anonymous

"YES!
And to those who sit.
To meditate."
Anxious Response.

draw. color. curse.
create. erase.
this is my space to
reflect on this lesson.

Hippie Handbook Lesson 21:

Setbacks

"Recovery. Recovery. Setback. Recovery.
Yeah, that is about how it went."

Remember way back in lesson one? When we were talking about life and healing not being a straight line. Well, we have come full circle in this journal. A setback when you are healing from anxiety, especially the first one you experience, can really throw you for a loop! But please know it is all part of the recovery process.

Unfortunately, there is no good time for a setback. And they usually hit you when you are doing really well and you think you have finally found your way out of the anxiety mess. And then BOOM! You feel like you are back at square one. And it hurts. It sucks. But I want you to know, you could never be back at square one- you have all this knowledge now and understanding about anxiety!!! A setback is just a moment in time. No more than that. You have the tools and the know-how on what to do to get yourself out of it.

Have you experienced a set-back already? How did it make you feel? Write about that here

_____

_____

_____

_____

_____

Sometimes setbacks can really put you in a spiral. Just know a setback lasts only as long as you allow it to. Let me repeat that because it is so important: a setback's length is directly related to how you respond to it. If you choose to see it as a moment in time and nothing more- you will gracefully move forward quickly. If you get pissed off, curse at it, say you are quitting and things like "this shit doesn't work.", well, you may be sitting in your setback for some time.

Here is a little checklist to help you focus on getting out of the setback quickly.

setback check-in

A CHECK IN FOR A SETBACK
REMEMBER IT IS PART OF THE PROCESS

- [ ] TAKE A DEEP BREATH
- [ ] REMEMBER YOU HAVE BEEN HERE BEFORE
- [ ] KNOW THIS IS TEMPORARY
- [ ] LOOK BACK AT YOUR PROGRESS
- [ ] HEALING IS NOT A STRAIGHT LINE
- [ ] BE GRATEFUL FOR THIS CHECK IN
- [ ] EAT SOME HEALTHY FOOD
- [ ] TAKE SOME TIME FOR EXERCISE
- [ ] GIVE THE STRESS TO GOD
- [ ] GET OUTDOORS AND SOAK IN THE SUN
- [ ] FORGIVE YOURSELF FOR SETBACK
- [ ] REMEMBER A GRATITUDE LIST
- [ ] MEDITATE AND BE IN THE PRESENT
- [ ] DO SOMETHING FUN
- [ ] LAUGH A FUCK TON

You got this! You are freaking awesome!

After reading the checklist, can you see a setback from a new perspective?

_____

_____

_____

_____

_____

What is your plan the next time you have a setback in your healing?

_____

_____

_____

_____

_____

Where is the humor in a setback? How can you see this from the lens of laughter? Can you see that there is humor in there somewhere? I would sing LL Cool J "Mama Said Knock You Out" song to know I was going to kick anxiety's ass, even in a setback! How can you see humor in this????

_____

_____

_____

_____

_____

Let's freaking wrap this lesson up!

Create up to three hashtags that sum up lesson 21 for you.
For example, in my book, the hashtag I created for this chapter is
#dontcallitasetback
What are yours?

\# _____

\# _____

\# _____

How are you feeling after that lesson?
Circle what you are feeling right now.
And it can be more than one!
Feelings are just that *feelings*
and they come and go.
Be honest with how you feel and allow yourself
to feel exactly where you are right now...

Feelin'   Feelin'   Feelin'   Feelin'   Feelin'   Feelin'   Feelin'
love   happy   groovy   okay   so sad   down   shit scared

"Every setback is a setup for a comeback."
-Joel Osteen

"And the comeback is going to be freaking brilliant!"
– Anxious Response

draw. color. curse.
create. erase.
this is my space to
reflect on this lesson.

Hippie Handbook Lesson 22:

Imperfect

"No one is immune to imperfection."

We are perfectly imperfect human beings.

And sometimes we may forget we are not meant to be perfect

So, this is the little reminder about perfection and healing.

The perfection healing definition:

"I will never have anxiety again. Zero symptoms. I can eat and drink whatever I want. And I am feeling good, smiling every fucking day."

The perfectly imperfect healing definition:

"I am doing my best. I love myself no matter what. If I feel good; great! If I feel shitty; I know how to get myself out of it. I celebrate my great days and I dance in the rain when things are a little off of center. It is all good. It is all God."

Reading these two definitions, what is your reaction? What feelings are coming up?

_____

_____

_____

_____

_____

A great analogy about healing from anxiety is the overflowing barrel or bucket.

Imagine a bucket. A bucket can only hold so much liquid until it overflows, right?

Okay. So, you are now healed from anxiety and you go back into some old habits, because who does not want to dive into chocolate cake???? And this snowballs into more sugary foods. And you stop exercising for a bit because you are busy eating cake... you understand where I am going with this.... it looks something like this...

How does your bucket overflow?
- Not getting enough sleep
- Letting in too much negative
- Eating food not good for me
- Not exercising
- List other ways for you here:
- ?
- ?
- ?

Can you list a few other ways that your bucket can overflow, even once you are "healed"? Write about that here.

_____

_____

_____

_____

_____

_____

And of course, from all the previous lessons, you absolutely know how to reduce the level in your bucket.

When you reduce the stressful activities, your bucket level lowers

- More sleep
- Spending time on postive activities
- Eating yummy, good food
- Walking, biking, etc...
- List other ways to reduce stress
- ?
- ?
- ?

What else would you do to reduce your bucket and help yourself get back to being symptom free?

_____

_____

_____

_____

_____

_____

Perfectly imperfect does not mean you will never heal from anxiety. It simply means that we are human and sometimes we go overboard one way and forget about balance. Okay, so what. We are not perfect. Cool. Now you know that when your bucket is full and you start experiencing symptoms you have the power to get out of it!

And guess what??? You have all the tools at your fingertips in this handbook!

You got this!

You have always had it!

I just helped you remember…

You are freaking amazing!!!

Let's freaking wrap this lesson up!

Create up to three hashtags that sum up lesson 22 for you.
For example, in my book, the hashtag I created for this chapter is
#partofthestory
What are yours?

 _____

_____

_____

How are you feeling after that lesson?
Circle what you are feeling right now.
And it can be more than one!
Feelings are just that *feelings*
and they come and go.
Be honest with how you feel and allow yourself
to feel exactly where you are right now...

Feelin'   Feelin'   Feelin'   Feelin'   Feelin'   Feelin'   Feelin'
love   happy   groovy   okay   so sad   down   shit scared

"Life isn't meant to be lived perfectly...but merely to be LIVED. Boldly, wildly, beautifully, uncertainly, imperfectly, magically LIVED."
-Mandy Hale

"Perfectly Imperfect is my new lens for life."
–Anxious Response

draw. color. curse.
create. erase.
this is my space to
reflect on this lesson.

✌Hippie Handbook Lesson 23:

Sharing Your Smile

"Helping others once you have helped your inside shine
is the best feeling ever"

Healing is not about the undoing of who you are. Because who you are, anxiety and all, is the secret sauce to your joy. Honestly. Every part of you is amazing and to try to sweep the "bad parts" under the rug and telling them to fuck off just brings the dust back up again one day to make for more anxiety.

Be you. Be authentically you. All this journal was about was allowing you, to be you, without the symptoms!

Once you feel good and have this shit down, please share what you have learned with others!

And not just what you have learned here, I mean your life, your gifts your amazingness-share it all. Because we really need that in the world. What you have to give is so important for us all.

Share kindness
Share love.
Share healing.
Share gifts.

What you do with this all is like a ripple effect for humanity. No shit. You are that amazing. Thank you for being you and washing off the lies of anxiety and shining bright and being a beacon for others! ✌️ ♡   🙏

You may believe you are just one drop in the ocean, but it is your action that creates a ripple effect for all.
Thank you!

YOU DID IT!
You completed
The Anxious Hippie Handbook.
CONGRATULATIONS!

the anxious hippie

Please shine brightly,
Lucie